21st Century
Basic Skills
Library

IT IS ABOUT TIME!

by Cecilia Minden, PhD

Cherry Lake Publishing • Ann Arbor, Michigan

1

CHERRY LAKE
Publishing

Published in the United States of America
by Cherry Lake Publishing
Ann Arbor, Michigan
www.cherrylakepublishing.com

Photo Credits: Cover and page 1, ©r.martens/Shutterstock, Inc.; page 4,
©iStockphoto.com/JoseGirarte; page 6, ©Nadezda/Shutterstock, Inc.;
page 8, ©Francesco Ridolfi/Shutterstock, Inc.; page 10, ©Hermínia Lúcia
Lopes Serra/Shutterstock, Inc.; page 12, ©Dmitriy Shironosov/Shutterstock,
Inc.; pages 14 and 16, ©Jacek Chabraszewski/Shutterstock, Inc.; page 18,
©Hal_P/Shutterstock, Inc.; page 20, ©get4net/Shutterstock, Inc.

Library of Congress Cataloging-in-Publication Data
Minden, Cecilia.
  It is about time!/by Cecilia Minden.
     p. cm.—(21st century basic skills Library. level 1)
  Includes bibliographical references and index.
  ISBN-13: 978-1-60279-847-2 (lib. bdg.)
  ISBN-10: 1-60279-847-8 (lib. bdg.)
  1. Time—Juvenile literature. 2. Time measurements—Juvenile literature.
I. Title. II. Series.
  QB209.5.M56 2010
  529—dc22   2009048566

Cherry Lake Publishing would like to acknowledge
the work of The Partnership for 21st Century Skills.
Please visit www.21stcenturyskills.org for more information.

Printed in the United States of America
Corporate Graphics Inc.
July 2010
CLFA07

TABLE OF CONTENTS

Tools We Use

Clocks help us tell time.

Little Hand

Little Hand

Clock **hands** show us the **hours** and **minutes**.

The little hand shows us the hour.

Look at the little hand.

What hour is it?

Big Hand

Big Hand

The big hand tells us the minutes.

There are 60 minutes in an hour.

The big hand is after the 12.

It is 5 minutes past 12 o'clock.

Now the big hand is before the 12.

It is 5 minutes before 12 o'clock.

Can you tell what time it is?

Look at the hands on the clock.

Did you say 10 minutes after 4 o'clock?

You are right!

What time is it now?

Find Out More

BOOK

Harris, Trudy. *The Clock Struck One: A Time-Telling Tale.*
  Minneapolis: Millbrook Press, 2009.

WEB SITE

Time for Time
www.time-for-time.com/game1.htm#
Play games that help you learn how to tell time.

Glossary

clocks (KLOKSS) tools used to measure time

hands (HANZ) tools on the face of clock that tell the hour
and minute

hours (AURZ) units of time; there are 24 hours in 1 day.

minutes (MIN-its) units of time; there are 60 minutes in 1 hour.

Home and School Connection

Use this list of words from the book to help your child become a better reader. Word games and writing activities can help beginning readers reinforce literacy skills.

after	hand	now	there
an	hands	o'clock	time
and	help	on	tools
at	hour	past	us
are	hours	right	use
before	in	say	we
big	is	show	what
can	it	shows	you
clock	little	tell	
clocks	look	tells	
did	minutes	the	

Index

About the Author

Cecilia Minden is the former Director of the Language and Literacy Program at the Harvard Graduate School of Education. She currently works as a literacy consultant for school and library publishers and is the author of more than 100 books for children.